Roots in the Air

MICHAEL HAMBURGER

Roots in the Air

Anvil Press Poetry

Published in 1991
by Anvil Press Poetry
69 King George Street London SE10 8PX

This book is published
with financial assistance from
The Arts Council of Great Britain

Photoset in Ehrhardt
by Saxon Computing, Derby
Printed in England
by the Arc & Throstle Press
Todmorden, Lancs

A catalogue record for this book
is available from the British Library

AUTHOR'S NOTE AND ACKNOWLEDGEMENTS

. Although essentially this is a collection of my poems written since
· 1983, the year in which I put together most of those written up to
that time for my *Collected Poems*, a degree of overlap or duplication
has arisen from two circumstances. The first is that I never know in
advance for how long I shall be working on any one sequence or
complex of inter-related poems, like the tree poems here which, in
theme at least, make a group, though the earliest of them go back to
1978 and were included in the *Collected Poems*. The second is that,
out of the same uncertainty, I did not withhold such poems either
from the *Collected Poems* or from the later *Selected Poems*. My main
acknowledgement, therefore, must be to Carcanet Press, who
published both these books, for allowing me to place a few older
poems in the sequence to which they now seem to belong. The tree
poems were also gathered separately for a limited edition, with
wood engravings by R. Samaraweera, by Roy Watkins in his
Embers Handpress in 1988; but even this gathering did not prove
definitive, and I have added a few unplanned and unexpected late-
comers to its contents.

Once again I have separated my dream poems from the rest,
because they need to be read in a different way; but even that
division is not without its problems. The poem called 'A Dream of
Water', for instance, also had its genesis in a dream; but because it
incorporates material from my waking life, or conscious memories
of it, as the others do not, I placed it in a different section.

A sardonic character called Mr Littlejoy, who appeared in three
poems in the early seventies, has also popped up again; and he turns
out to be no more consistent or predictable than my other voices or
modes.

As for acknowledgements to periodicals and anthologies, these
are bedevilled both by the overlap and my inability to keep a
complete record of first publications. I should not list them at all if
certain editors had not asked me specifically to do so. Any omission
there may be for poems first published after 1983 is due to gaps in
the record. Because a few of my later poems first appeared in
foreign periodicals, either in the original or in translation, I include
acknowledgements to these.

My thanks are due to the editors of the following magazines and anthologies: *Agenda*, *Argo*, ASSEMBLAGE (University of Essex), BENEATH THE WIDE HEAVEN, *Hubbub* (USA), IMAGES FOR AFRICA, *Lines Review*, *Neue Zürcher Zeitung* (Switzerland), *Oxford Magazine*, POETRY BOOK SOCIETY ANTHOLOGY 1986/7, 1988/9, *Poetry Canada Review*, *Poetry Ireland Review*, *Poetry Review*, *PN Review*, POLY (USA), *The Rambler* (Uzès, France), *Resurgence*, *The Rialto*, *Scripsi* (Australia), *Signal* (USA), *Southern Humanities Review* (USA), *Stand*, THE EXPERIENCE OF LANDSCAPE (Arts Council of Great Britain), THISTLEDOWN (UNICEF, Ireland), VOICES IN THE GALLERY (Tate Gallery), WAS SPRACHE IST? (Der Prokurist, Austria), WITH A POET'S EYE (Tate Gallery) and *Die Zeit* (Germany).

CONTENTS

I

II

I
Trees

WILLOW

Hard wood or soft?
It is light, startlingly,
Not close-grained, to last
As oak does; but makes up
In obstinate wiry toughness for that
With all its fibres.
From the barkless bough
My axe rebounds;
My handsaw bends,
From the sham death
Willow, by shamming, defies.

Pick any twig, dormant
Or wrenched off in a gale,
Stick it in moist earth,
And it makes a tree.
Leave a trunk, fallen
Or felled, sprawling
Across a stream,
And it lives on,
Sprouts from the hollow
Half-rotten stump or
Takes root from a dropped limb.

Chop up the dry remains,
Burn them: they'll spit.

ELM

Here since the Ice Age, not long ago
In girth, height, it could match
Linden or beech, and by abundance of leaves,
Minuscule, crinkled, was potent.
If, weak in the joint, a limb could drop,
It had more, pushed out its progeny
Of suckers near and far
To possess all the land they could grab,
Leathery-skinned from the start,
The wood unyielding, hard,
Not fragrant even in death.

Yet picked on, and not by us,
For a feast that kills,
Food for a beetle, a fungus
Colluding as never before,
One by one, though slowly,
The great trees lay bare
White boles, shedding
Their knobbed and ridged bark
Till the last bough starves.
One by one the corpses
Are felled and burnt
By us, their undertakers.

But a root can live on,
Through hedgerow or field thrust
New stems with twigs that will swell
Buds of that curled leaf still.

BEECH

Starve, cramp the root,
Lop the trunk, closely set it in rows
And the trees will deny themselves,
Make a hedge for you, tamed,
Renouncing the girth and height
That, free, centenarian, in field
Or park they could swell to – their planters
Long left behind, outgrown. They will keep then
Their dry, brown leafage
All winter, until the crinkled
Ribbed silk of new leaves pushes
Away the deathly cover
No gale could remove;
Yet strain mightily,
Sideways and up, for growth,
Putting out limbs that shine
With a bronze lacquer too smooth
For bark; and, unless cut back,
Must kill or die, so straitened.

From the cuttings, though moist,
Live still, fire will draw
A joss-stick fragrance;
From thwarted, rotten tinder
Kingfisher flames, a flaring
Of brightest blue-greens
Before the white ashes
Let winds have their way.

HAWTHORN

Poignantly praised in Proust's
Long periods as blossom only,
And fragrance at that, diffused
In air as purely vernal
As memories of the famous month
That gave it one of its names –
When now springs creep in
By the day, the hour, and reverse
Or hold back until June,
That blossom, handled or smelled
Close to, exhales no sweetness
But a rank putridness rather –
By selective culture, true,
Of pink to red flowers, it can serve
As a park or garden tree
Of middling stature, pretty
As Japanese prunus, in season,
And redolent, from afar;
But by nature, all the year round,
Fittest for making a hedge
Proof against trespassing mammals,
Provider, diminished now,
Of nesting-sites for wrens,
Of haws for thrushes and finches;
And wilder, self-seeded,
Crookedly straggling sideways
Under cover of tall grass,
Or its lobed leaves in hedgerows
Mistaken for those of the blander
Field or Montpellier maple,
Down the ages it has been cursed
In every un-Proustian vernacular
When under thumbnails it drove
Its needle-sharp spikes.

BIRCH

Vestal she seems, ballerina
Of wildest, of waste places,
With an aspiration to whiteness
Fulfilled in America's North,
A papery peel so flawless,
It would shame the contagion of ink;
Yet rarely will attain
Her maturity's fullness,
Too often herself wasted,
Her bitter, her harsh timber
Stunted by what she favours,
Blizzards bending her limbs,
Long stillness under snow;
Will lie prone suddenly,
Crowded out, or as though felled
By a blow from her own boughs.
And proves brittle then, graceless:
Her wrapping of bark more lasting
Than the mouldered body within.

ELDER

Tree-sized weed that, allowed to prosper,
Will impersonate ash
From a distance at least
And in leaf only, before
It puts on blossom or berry,
A blushing white or a blackish crimson
From its imposture of branches
Whose marrow is pith, or nothing,
With a weed's impudence, elder,
Bird-seeded, will crop up
Anywhere, useful to birds
As to human consumers able,
By fermentation, to draw
From the dry flower, acrid pulp of the fruit
An essence pungently sweet.

Such use it permits
But punishes those
Taken in by its would-be timber
To burn it indoors.
I did, and learned:
Taken in, for burning,
One felled intruder yielded
Little brightness, less heat,
But a perfume compounded
Of sulphur and cabbage,
A nauseous blend.
Worse, my favourite pipe
Dropped for no reason, the stem,
Hollow too, not of good wood either,
Irreparably snapped.

Call it shrub, then, or scrub
Where too rankly it upstarts,
But give it room, if you can,
For a lavish pretending,
For a wealth of moon umbels
Darkening, waning through purple to black.

BALSAM POPLAR

As a sucker, mere stick, awry,
This one was found and uprooted,
Took to the place, and within five years,
True, straight, it has risen
Not at the rate of the Lombardy
Whose one aspiration is to become
A landmark, leaving the slower oaks
To compete for breath, dwarfed as cottages are
By the church spire; but puts out instead
Lateral boughs, leafage larger and longer
Which, in bud and new, exhales
A jonquil sweetness, as though
It needed no flowers to fulfil itself,
Sterile perhaps, until
The roots, mature, can provide for offspring.

So fragrant, it seems exotic,
Yet after a winter that killed and lingered
Is more forthcoming than its more common kin,
The white and the black, still bare;
Sturdier, too, in its fibre and shape,
Lets go of no branch or leaf
In a gale, nor jitters like aspen.

Never yet having gathered
One fallen twig, for burning,
Nor lopped or chopped its timber,
I cannot tell where the sweetness begins,
Whether in wood cells, engrained,
Whether distilled out of acrid earth
Or only at the tips, by a marriage with air.

FIG

London made this one: it germinated
On a compost heap, from a matrix
Desiccated and old –
Some fig-end chucked out as refuse;
From a flower-pot began its ascent into light,
A stowaway there, so strange, it was welcome
And planted out. Then dug up, transported
To a colder county, with gales from the North Sea,
Where, rooted in shingle, it took, and throve,
Put out great five-fingered leaves;
Barren, after ten years, but far from mature.

Against a wall even colder, facing east,
Another grows, its genesis and rearing,
From stock long naturalized, all coddled, planned:
Its foliage smaller, gently lobed, more rounded.
When, after springs that ripped or froze their blossom,
Plum, pear and apple fail, this tree bears fruit,
Holds on to them till, purpled ripe, they droop;
Concealed its flowering, needed no bee,
Saw its fruit nodules all the way through winter.

Foundling or nursling, more or less hardened,
From base to leaf-rim fig has a single nature:
Not to set wood, but by a rubbery smoothness
Husband resources, make the most of weather,
Nor, till the seed sweetens, let its thick skin crack.

YEW

Too slowly for us it amasses
Its dense dark bulk.
Even without our blood
For food, where mature one stands
It's beyond us, putting on
Half-inches towards its millennium,
Reaching down farther
Than our memories, our machines.
Its fertile berries can kill.
Its dead wood even, still harsh,
In gate-post or bedstead
Outlasts many users
Of gates, of beds.
Woodworm, bedbug avoid it,
Those who used it said.

If one tree stands, black,
Where many trees were
And they whose counter-nature
For all things had a use
Till unburied their flesh littered
The used, the flayed earth,
A yew it will be, split,
Thrusting down slow roots,
Millennial, still to where
Soil remains whole.

OAK

Slow in growth, late in putting out leaves,
And the full leaves dark, austere,
Neither the flower nor the fruit sweet
Save to the harsh jay's tongue, squirrel's and boar's,
Oak has an earthward urge, each bough dithers,
Now rising, now jerked aside, twisted back,
Only the bulk of the lower trunk keeps
A straight course, only the massed foliage together
Rounds a shape out of knots and zigzags.

But when other trees, even the late-leaved ash,
Slow-growing walnut, wide-branching beech and linden
Sway in a summer wind, poplar and willow bend,
Oak alone looks compact, in a stillness hides
Black stumps of limbs that blight or blast bared;
And for death reserves its more durable substance.

On wide floorboards four centuries old,
Sloping, yet scarcely worn, I can walk
And in words not oaken, those of my time, diminished,
Mark them that never were a monument
But plain utility, and mark the diminution,
Loss of that patient tree, loss of the skills
That matched the patience, shaping hard wood
To outlast the worker and outlast the user;
How by oak-beams, worm-eaten,
This cottage stands, when brick and plaster have crumbled,
In casements of oak the leaded panes rest
Where new frames, new doors, mere deal, again and again
    have rotted.

A MISALLIANCE

'Strange, strange. How can it be?'
My friend said, calling me to his garden
To see a hybrid, symbiotic sapling –
A present, he explained, for the betrothal
Whose very celebration broke it off,
So that to a severance his guests had drunk.

The tree he'd planted as a mountain ash
Or rowan, *sorbus aucuparia*,
On one of its twin trunks
Bore quite another leaf,
Not lanceolate, serrated
But oval, larger, thicker, lobed,
With more than the dusting of silver
Of the rowan leaf's underside:
A *sorbus*, too, I half-recognized
But forgot the name: *intermedia*,
The Swedish whitebeam.

Traced down, both appeared to rise
From the same rootstock, branching.
Whether by graft or mere compression joined,
Only a going to the root could show.
I feared it was a grafting
Beyond my skill to undo,
Once dubious art had become nature.

But I confirmed: together they could not grow,
Feed and develop on their narrow plot
Even if without surgery one could be saved there.

Which, was his choice alone,
Because, no broker, breaker, lawyer of such marriage
Nor psychotherapist, in that I would not meddle.

Oh, and the prodigy had begun to turn
Too sinister, now that foreboding told me
The choice that he would make:
To rid himself of both, expunge the token,
Uproot them, coupled in a double death.

A TREE'S DYING

Before six one August morning, the dewfall heavy,
The air still, we are wrenched awake
By a creak and thump that could be
The beams of our house breaking up.
But silence mends: we are safe.
It had happened before, last year:
One of the four great limbs
Of the tall white willow fallen
With all its burden of massed wet leaves;
Then months of labour, of dragging, sawing, chopping
After first aid to the bruised or maimed
Smaller trees it had struck.

Not quite released from the trunk's fork,
Now another sprawls, leans on the bent boughs,
On the snapped, of poplar and birch,
So bulky in ruin, it makes a wall
That, left, would possess, transform
More than the strip it covers; and, willow,
Deny its death, somehow strike root again
From a fibre that loves to live:
Corpse and sapling at once, take over.

And the torso – alive or dead?
Doomed, the remaining two limbs
That, in turn forked, still rise
From the trunk's fork, decayed?

As long as they bear leaves,
We'll not presume, though threatened,
But let their dying be
Slow as the tree's growing

That, halved, still shall stand
And may not thud again
While we, who did not plant it,
Weather-fended, sleep here and wake.

A MASSACRE

(17th October 1987)

It came like judgement, came like the blast
Of power that, turned against itself, brings home
Presumption to the unpresuming also,
To those who suffered power and those unborn.

In the small hours
We woke to it, a howling, lashing
That rocked the house; then, muffled
By the closed, curtained windows, crashes, cracks,
Far off or near. We did not rise
And did not peer, but listened
Into the darkness even when overhead
Things hurtled, burst or boomed,
But in the havoc coupled, as though to pit
One wholeness, though the last we had, against
So general a fission, and lay unmoved
Till daybreak roused us from our drowsing,
While still the hurricane rushed,
Half-light allowed a hesitant half-looking.

She saw what, before action, my sight refused,
Fearful because she loved it best,
Went straight to it in mind, the mulberry tree,
Straight to the space its bunched and knotted mass
Down to the lawn had filled, the low boughs propped
On rests made for them by a gardener dead,
Not for our tenure, lest their own weight break them.
These only upright now; the sound, live growth
Of centuries undone
By the roots' wrenching, the full foliage withered,
Curled round no fruit that had been lately sweet
Within the woody roughness of its fibre.

And while the gale swept on,
Beyond the dawn's, no light marked farm or village,
She met another absence, at the lawn's far edge,
Pyramid of the larch that leaned, not sprawled
From rootwork, a mere decade's, partly ripped
Out of the soil a rainy year had softened;
Yet grown too tall and wide for us to raise,
Lever from sure starvation, though its drooping
Girdled a rarer sapling, purple maple
Endangered by more subsidence, when the fall
Had neither bent nor rent it.

This was for later finding, later care
Among the lack and wreckage that she sensed
Before the morning brightened
And we went out.
Already, too, her care had found its way
To larger emptiness, left by the Lombardy poplar
Gone from the eastern sky,
Live column, fluttering spire so tall
That miles away on walks they'd shown us home;

Only the longest, though, of the tree corpses
Lying across the marsh
With ramparts now of great root clusters
And loam, their matrix, raised on the dyke's bank;
New pools inside it, scooped from its bed;
New wilderness along it, tangle of trunks and limbs –
Ash, linden, birches, plane, and the white poplar
Less set on rising than the Lombardy,
Its greater bulk and girth stopped in their fall
By a slim cable pole, therefore to be dismembered,
Cut to the stump, mocking memorial
No one will need where a whole skyline gapes,
Beyond our ravaged acre and world-wide
A slow or sudden killing
Comes to the trees like judgement, not on them.

Until the mended house
Is hit again by worse than any weather
Its beams of oak withstood,
Dead wood still older than the mulberry,
Though sheltered by whichever trees remain
Of those we tended, planted or let be,
The beech not toppled, or self-seeded hawthorn,
Sycamore, elder, scrub of the blighted elm,
Our work is clearance, unremembering
And unforeknowing, too,
For what resurgence, change or progeny
The labour will make room,
What of the lumber burned and what removed,
What, by discarding, we give back to roots
As food for leafage, food for whose need of leaves.

More emptiness, then. Now to be filled
Less by our choosing, less by one grain, one savour,
One shape accepted only or loved best
Among those made by air, earth, water, fire
In multiple mutation, fusion, fission,
Than by their bare subsistence that's our own;
And light above all, as long as light will shine.

EPILOGUE

(November)

Thanks to good neighbours and their tractor's arm,
Backed up by stake and rope,
Straight, scarcely lopped, the larch stands, yellowing,
Shedding its needles as the month demands –
Whether to bud or perish, spring will tell.

The mulberry lies and looms: from its short trunk
That kneels now, on one stump,
Two limbs, one thick and forked, one slender, rise,
Near enough upright to look tree-like still,
Thanks to its nature only,
All devious, spiralling, its crooked ways –
Whether with roots enough in earth, not air
(Or fire by now) to burgeon, spring will tell,
Even in death its knobby bole outlast
Our tenure and our eyes,
A few twigs dither as they did, though bare;
At worst a ruin, useless, like those built
For the splenetic owners of large houses
Too comfortable for them, too secure
In parks too much their own: *memento mori*,
At best the living relic of a tree
That, not for us, could make a mulberry.

Sweetly meanwhile its timber, chopped or sawn,
Hisses on household grates
Where, mixed with lesser pickings from the slaughter,
The work and hope of many seasons yield
Warmth for one season, bucketsfull of ash
Doled out to the survivors, less in hope
Than wintry patience now, numbed expectation:
Here and for us no linden will surprise
Harsh land with fragrance from loose button flowers

Unnoticed under leaves that seemed as plain
Till, fully leafed, it fell.
For other growth we clear the ground and wait.

Today a new gale whistles through the marsh,
Strips to the skeleton trees live and dead
But brings none down. The sun shines. All is well.

AFTERLIVES

(1990)

Rid of the counterweight, the width and height,
Lumber of one life's growing,
Roots in the air, wrapped in a dole of earth,
Plunged back into their matrix.

Pollarded now, a dotterel, the plane
Out of its crippling makes a resurrection,
With roundness, fulness, density of leafage
Transcends the loss of limbs and crest lopped off;
In its contraction still can drink and breathe,
Wear on the torso, too, the bark's own markings.

Cut to a stump, the linden feeds
A nursery of stemlets
And as a bush commemorates the tree,
Perpetuates its leaf that, larger now,
Asserts the simple heart-shape, the near-circle,
If not to rise or blossom, to live on.

Prostrate, the mulberry from half its roots,
Far less than half its wood of centuries,
Shoots again, grapples, twists
And on the old as on the new twigs bears
Fruit for the blackbirds, thrushes,
With luck a few for us;
Who now, more singly seeing, meet what remains,
Less than the tree it was and more than a tree
By the diminishment, the lying low,
Bedded on grass, with poppies and balsam lush
Where the shade was its greater prospering cast.

II

TO BRIDGE A LULL

i.m. George Oppen

Alone in your genus, ectopistes,
Your flocks were thunder clouds
That discharged themselves on forests,
Clattering down, breaking thick branches
With the weight of your roosts or nests
When you broke your journeys, rested.
In thousands then you were slaughtered,
Smoked out with sulphur, clubbed
Or shot on acres white
With your acid dung. So many
That herds of pigs were turned loose
To fatten on carcasses left
When their keepers, Indian, colonist,
Had bagged all they could eat.
At a mile a minute, billionfold,
Long-tailed and purple-necked,
Powerful flyers, you travelled
Between Mexico and Quebec,
Able to rear, it was thought,
At any season, wherever
Abundance of fruit or seed
Matched your multiple hunger,
One male, one female, and those
Mature within half a year.
And then you were gone;
And then in tens, not thousands
Were seen again and counted;
And then were not seen again.

Ectopistes. Vagrants. A dead name I write
To bridge a lull. Absurdly let
Lips, tongue that will be dumb
Address what is not, never could make out

The spoken or the written vocable, dead.
And hear the clatter still,
Come down to ravage forests razed
By your self-ravaging destroyers
Whose obsolescent words I write.
And see the sky blacked out
Not where your millions passed,
Light breaking as you hurtled to escape
Eagle or hawk, armed with their talons only,
But by a larger, lingering darkness that's unbroken.
A stillness, cold, your kind could share with mine
Fills with your flocks, absurdly
Brings back what dead men called you, passenger.

WINTER JASMINE

For a cold blossoming, less than cold praise:
Under veiled skies, in greyness
Eyes too are veiled,
And invisible almost against
A wall too much haze cast adrift
Nor weighty with fragrance as
Of its white kin
Or winter-white viburnum, honeysuckle,
To an absence of bees
It lavishly opens, displays
All those mock-suns, in vain;
Shines, but for senses dormant
Till aconite
With surprise caps its yellow
That fades now, dies.

WINTER ACONITE, ADONIS

Not ostentatious either, long before
The trumpeted daffodils
Make spring official, but so small
That one must know the patch, clear it of sodden grass
To see the curled stalks bear
Furled yellow into still forbidding air
Of this last January day,
Opening only when the sun gets through
Or never, should the drizzle and the mist
Forbiddingly persist.
Furled or unfurled, foreknown or unforeknown,
By sheer anachronism more they will surprise
Than snowdrop white that's wintry to our eyes;
And before snowdrops may have come and gone –

Unlike adonis, built to last, defy
All sorts of weather, by holding back
The sturdier blossom on the sturdier stalk
For weeks, or months if need be, cunningly,
Leafage wrapped round it, and a tinge of green
Outside the yellow petals, for disguise,
Unfurling, furling, till true warmth sets in.
Then let the fanfares blare,
The pampered pomp of frilly daffodils blaze!
Its work is done, in frost's and wind's despite,
To put on death now, sweet
While all and sundry feast on the easier air.

WINTER HONEYSUCKLE

i.m. Elizabeth Smart

White as hoarfrost, whiter than ice,
In hoarfrost, ice its floweret petals open
For what angelic bees to pollinate –
Night-flying bees, inaudible and white?
As though white-pillowed in white sheets, and white
Not only smiling a dead face could lie
But take and leave no break,
No season's growth retracted, not one day disowned.
Nor, in snow flurries, leafless:
Fragrant from shoots all fleshed and newly spread despite
Air that seems deathly too, deep-frozen ground.

MIGRANTS II

Once more they gather, swallows and martins,
On the wires along the lane.
This time, laid up with wear in the joints,
Through a window I see them,
Our plot receding from me
Before it's empty of them who more surely always
Than whitethroat or willow warbler have marked
Summer for us, cutting through sharpest winds,
Sitting out thunderstorm, tacking in rain
To home again with their twitter
Under rafter, eaves, for the first or the second brood.

The husk of one martin fledgling
Hangs from its mud-nest's rim:
Passed on, with no straining of wings.

Coldly housed here, as on either passage,
Always they're going home.

MIGRANTS III

Hardly this year I'd looked up
When swifts streaked over, shrieking,
Who hate the rooftops they skim,
Never, alive, will rest there
Yet belong to our day.

Hardly had listened
To the mutter above
The morning window,
Noted the homing
And sorties of martins,
Counted their repossessed
And empty nests;
Only high up, in clear skies,
Followed their flutter and glide
Till as bobbing dots they blurred.

Hardly the loops, dives,
Fewer, of swallows
To their dank nesting-place
I might have doubted but
For their droppings, new
On the woodpile beneath it;
Wholly had missed
Their congregations on wires,
Rehearsals for departure.

Now it's the rarer grace:
Glimpsed flock of goldfinch
Feeding on thistle seed;
Of long-tailed titmouse
In dipping flurry
From copse to copse:
A different nearness,

Farness, beyond our need
For recurrence, return.

Seeing one swallow,
Left behind, fly low
Close to the cropped meadow,
One martin rise between
Willows green still and full,
All at once I hear
A silence that's autumn,
An absence in the air.

A WALK IN THE COTSWOLDS

with Frances Horovitz

Moon-pale even there, in the valley
She'd learnt by heart, showing me marjoram
Wild and abundant as common grasses,
So lightly she stepped, I thought
She'd never need more of earth
Than the pull of it, against
An urge less to rise than to hover.

But 'flowers became stone',
Her lunar nature weighted
With love, for a man, a child
And a place that would hold them, hold her,

Till she hovered again, heavier,
Pulled this way and that, wrenched;
And for healing must hurtle down.

CASE

for my sister Maria,
'saved' by a brain operation

In a language tongueless –
Her tongue is paralysed –
From below her punctured throat,
In a language toothless –
Teeth were extracted lest
They bite the tongue
That has not tasted, spoken
These eight hundred days
But once had sung –
From beneath dumbness she draws,
All too clear, the one plea
Of what they left of her:
'I want to die'.

Then her mouth gapes, inane.
Then her head drops on to
The one limb that could serve her
If there were anything
A moving arm could do
For what they left of her,
If there were anything
For a lone arm to do.

Nothing her touched hand says.
Nothing her face, raised,
Nothing now the draughts
From a well too deep.

For a hint, a glint of brightness
That I might recognize
I search her eyes,
Unanswering, and read:

'Nothing. Not here. Not here.
Broken the circuit, the ring
That makes your light the day's,
Your darkness night's.
From either, mine by rights,
They severed me;
To the detritus, shame,
Give sustenance and a name.

Remembrance? Oh, enough
To know I am destroyed.
Feeling enough to sense
My senses' impotence,
Suffer the void.
Hearing enough to shun
Music that would convey
Only what's lost to me,
Relation, harmony.

One question. Only one:
Surgeon, what have you done?
What science blessed your knife,
Calls life this dereliction,
Life-saving, life-support
The cold retort
That fills me up with fuel.
Think, you whose brains are whole,
Beyond your skill more cruel
Than fiercest hate or rage
Stabbing to kill.
Or else, computer-ruled,
Computer-fooled,
Implant your electronics
Where mind was, and restart
Your engine's pump, the heart.

My keepers, if I could,
If I were I enough

To weep or smile or laugh,
To speak a word,
I'd thank you for your care.
From half-light all my own
Where those I loved are shadows
Into the dark they'll share,
Into the flash that blinds
Past you I stare.'

RELEASE

When at last it seemed
That, breath itself blocked,
Delirious, she might elude
Their drugs, their needles, their tubes,
In half-dream's eye
A young woman walked
Through a spinney of birch and beech
Newly leaved – she
Who for years had not walked,
And the month November
With birch-leaves yellow,
Beech-leaves russet-gold –
Towards a great boulder
Whose oval split
And opened, hollow.

Never turning her head
Back to the play
Of sunbeams, cloud shadows,
As she would her own house
Left unlit, unlocked,
Unchanged, she entered it.

IN LONDON I

Once I thought I was centred
Here, at the heart of a compass rose,
And the needle quivered
Between too many districts and doors.

Now I sit in a little park
A few streets west of the house where my father died –
Blasted by bombs, then demolished;
A few streets east of the house where my mother died –
Refurbished by strangers, with a gable added
To the garage used for no car of hers
In her widowhood's forty years.

Roses have shed their petals,
Only the stigma holds, but not here:
On to the park bench
Whole blossoms fall,
Crimson-cored white, from a hibiscus tree,
And buds that by tomorrow
Will have been swept from the flagstones.

One sister's at work in a different borough.
One daughter's at work in another.
A few friends remain in rooms I remember,
In streets recognizable still.

Too deep in his then, there,
An old man stares unseeing.
Beside him grandmothers gossip
Or watch the toddlers at play,
Au pair girls from anywhere,
A sun-bathing couple, quiet
Within the traffic of circling prams –

Islanded, islanded all,
And each island adrift,
Every shoreline shifting.

Beyond these voices,
The low, the loud, beyond
The more distant noises, dampened
By housefronts, by shrubs,
And the silence an old man keeps,
I hear sea waves break.

AGING

It is a return, with the luggage lighter,
Some of it lost, though it held the snapshots, notes
But for whose evidence none could be sure
Where he has been, the traveller come home.
Hardly himself, rid of the clutter,
More lithe for that in mind, in limb the heavier
For having dragged belongings yet again
From house to train, station to station,
From train to airport, counter to gate,
From airport to new lodging,
Sleep wrung from strange street noises, on a rented bed.
There's not room in one heart, one head
For the ten times ten thousand things.

Winter light, then, on a field grown barer,
Some of the great trees rotted, some cut to the stump.
Plainsong once more, after polyphony
That clotted, cloyed the ear and died of richness.
Within a single line, the length and depth
Of all past seeing now, past hearing,
Concert of absent voices, instruments;
And in one faint unseasonable breath
Essence of what the winds of many seasons carried
Across the frontiers, shores,
Parallel, solstice, turning of eras, years.

WITH A GIFT OF GRAPES

No need for names between us.
For years you were no more
Than the 'little old man in the old house' –
Oldest, they say, in the village street,
With a bold front still
In weathered red brick holding good
For you and for anyone
Because that is all they will see of it
As long as you're there to defend the door
From prying prospectors, inspectors –
Who almost won when a tree had pushed
Through two floors and the attic
Till the crest, in its element
And free again as you are in dereliction and loss
Triumphantly waved green leaves.

No need either ever to let me in,
Though the roses they call old-fashioned
Around the same door made us friends
When I stopped to ask you their names –
Never yet found or needed, since cuttings of them
Are striking roots in our garden;
Oh, and another too,
Darkest red and old-fashioned, compacted,
From the back of your house, the plot
Never seen and rumoured to be
Rain forest rather than garden.

'Only a little low bush', you apologized
When you brought cuttings, with one late flower,
One bud that might open still –
Little and low, like all our exchanges
And nameless again, Mr D.,
Who worked as a gardener once

But now make do with narrowest needs
In the little space your means or labour can wrest
From dilapidation, leakage and wilderness;
Yet keep that space your own
By grace of her who left you the use of it
While a roof of sorts is needed.

Here's another return
Of the tokens we exchange
In the narrowing space we share,
You in your house, I in mine,
With brief meetings outside them –
Words that may not take
Any more than cuttings, may not outlast
Your roses, the climbers, the bush,
Little and low, darkest red.
All will be bulldozed surely
When we are gone. It's the knowledge
Of that our exchanges mean
Behind words and names;
And the freedom, the joy
Of needing less and less,
Needing to know less and less.

IN LONDON II

for Claire

Housing love, that is hard enough,
Both for children and for another making
In disorder to give it a base, a place;
Harder still, though, to lavish it homeless,
Shapes and music and words running loose
For the sake of community, healing.

Main street, market affirm a commingling of needs,
And for progress there's traffic along them;
Not the cinema's gutted hulk,
Side street hiding abandoned workshops,
Boarded windows, doorways that frame a darkness,
Best endeavour shamed by the plain clean lines
Of the ancient alms-house grown alien, remote.

On the bus, from his mother's lap
More than once the little black boy reaches out
For the book a stranger is reading,
Grieves when the pages are turned.
She, the reader, is kind, but the book will close.

Less confined than most, the rabbit in your back yard,
Though unmated, leaves you no plant that can flower,
Freely ranging there, still is thwarted,
For subsistence held within bounds of the given,
For fulfilment driven to break those bounds.
So, picked up to be fondled, he clawed
Your small daughter, punishing your love through hers.

As I limp through Hackney, a visitor merely,
Lamed elsewhere, on grounds that look different,
What to you can I say of setbacks, who live
Where the poor are punished for paining the better-off

And unease, become hate, has knotted the law for lashing?
What of love that defies them, my stubborn daughter?
Only that between us which needs no saying:
All's despite, all our making a making-do.

There we meet again, with a home in common.

ANOTHER IRISH QUESTION

to Dennis and Julie

What county was it, what place
Between Galway and Dublin where, stopping
For one-night lodging we lugged
Our intimate baggage and dreams?
Waking from conversation with our own dead
To plastic flowers, framed saints,
The Virgin Mary in painted plaster,
An odour not of sanctity but of damp dust
And worse from the wardrobe never cleared
Of the widowed landlady's husband
Whose toothbrush and razor, too,
Remained enshrined, in the bathroom?
But small-talk so bright was served
With the porridge and rare-boiled egg?

SONG AND SILENCE

Variations on a theme
of Walther von der Vogelweide
(c. 1170–1230)

The doubters say that everything is dead,
And no one living who can make a song.
Let them consider well the common dread,
How all the world grapples with grievous wrong.
When song's day dawns, such verse and song they'll hear
As will make them wonder.
I heard a little bird lament the self-same fear,
Sheltering from thunder:
'I will not sing till the black skies clear.'

I

In megapolitan gardens, on the land
When air was innocent things heard were true:
Wild birds that condescended to a hand,
For sustenance they perched before they flew
Back into strangeness, a brief juncture broken;
And then, wild words, absconded into song
Where they, not feeding hand or mind, belong.

No words remain but tab-words drably spoken
By managers of aviaries, or the air,
To cage, with expert care,
And safeguard from the toxins that can kill
Residual singing birds,
Residual singing words
Which, huddled now in lines too long, are still,
Showing their keepers what their keepers know:
That they have made it so,
A counter-world dependent on their skill.
Here wings are folded, truthful voices low.

II

Midwinter, but because the days are mild
In grey light missel-thrush and robin sing.
We too, whose weather is remembering,
Not only out of season,
Against it if we cannot sing must mutter,
For soon it will be treason
To doubt the soundness of our commondearth
Whose *ultima ratio* is the death of earth;
Before the reasoners in their money-madness
Choke all the springs of gladness,
With their machines and machinations clutter
Natural song, the human and the wild.

If dying swans break silence, so can we,
If they keep faith, who have no memory
Beyond their inborn need
Of water, air and weed,
The fire in us, now banked with dampening care,
Must feed on that which smothers it, to flare,
Blaze for the sake of brightness,
Though there are those whom no plain fire will sear
Into a sense of rightness;
Nor in our lifetime will the black clouds clear.

III

So in the end we find what in the end
Is privilege beyond all tampering,
An openness of sky
Only at times the swooping aircraft rend,
A place in which to die
As poisoned birds do, but till then take wing,
Impelled to flight by every earthly thing
The tamperers could reach and nullify.

From sickened air, shore of a sea grown foul
Still skies of any colour set us free
In mind at least to follow
Larks into glare or into dusk the owl,
From a dark room the swallow –
Or ghost of each, the mere trajectory
More sure than man-made missile's course can be
That homes to no inhabitable hollow.

Horizon tree-lined, roof-marked, concrete-cliffed,
But in our lowlands large enough for eyes
To rest on or to roam;
As a last garden, clouds the wind will shift,
Light flowers not fed by loam,
Nor labour, when from shorter sleep we rise
To that residual property, the skies
Louder by then, though birdless, but a home.

AT THE ASSUMPTION OF JOHN CLARE
TO WESTMINSTER ABBEY

To walk four nights, three days with one good shoe –
That he got through,
Sustained by chewed tobacco and plucked grass:
Such trials pass.
And, walking, let your fancies, wishes drift –
Small slide, small shift.
Cut off, to a dead son convey your love,
That they call madness
Though absence is the only death we know
And live in that when into it they shove
One whom a different absence – elms laid low –
Had robbed of gladness.
In mind alone fit out his cottage farm –
That did him harm.
To love the dead girl like the living woman
And the dead son
Was to live on a little, almost human
When all was absent, absent every one.
Not hardship, illness did for you, John Clare,
But wear and tear,
And not on you but on the place and things
So much yourself that their diminishings
You could not bear.
For his remains in landmarks, leafage, wings
Go and look there.

PEACOCK

With all his finery, the sapphire, emerald
Dusted with gold, embossed with glowering purple,
The full regalia of a scattered lineage
He came to us, but as a refugee
From farm machinery, farm dogs that had mauled
His mate and killed her. For his day-time seat
Chose an old pear-tree so wrenched, so loosely rooted
It leans on air for a last blossoming.
There he bears bluster, downpour, never looking
For man-made shelter, lets the brilliance fade,
His gloss of feathers ruffle, the cold rain wash him.
Then does not strut but nods along the lawn,
Blotting their colours, drags his heavy train
Over the flowerbeds, pecks at honesty
But thrives on foxglove, poison to other breeds.

Wavily patterned in buff and black, his wings,
Rarely unfolded, are discreetly dapper,
Their pinions monochrome, rich earthy brown.
On his diminutive head the flimsy crown
Is lyre-shaped, lyre-stringed the tufts of those plumes
He'll spread for show despite his widowhood,
The fan's two hundred eyes not made for seeing
Which from a centre more compact, more golden,
Shiver and hiss, though in a light so muted
That they are lent no lustre not their own.
Will sway, will dance in step with her who's alien,
His host and keeper; then suddenly will turn
To her the splendour's risible underside,
Grey skeleton of its workings, at their hub
A patch of baby fluff, mere whitish down.

Plangent glissando, the smallest of his voices
Mingles with cockcrow, questions the day to come.

Still from his night-time vantage, a high limb
Of this tall ash-tree smooth and straight, but leafless,
It shames the small birds' habit of gladder song.
What now he celebrates, now mews, now moans,
Now screeches out is barest, mean survival.
He watches, rouses, warns; to our ears carries
Forest all felled that when it owned and matched him
His loudest voice could pierce, for company –

And even here, in marshland, pasture, field
Has found it, from a mile away has drawn
A phantom of himself, pale visitor
Who, formed as he is, lacks the interplay
Of mud shades with the peacock iridescence,
The markings, emblems we can no more make out
Than his weird modes of music, plaint or lure.

The ghostly bird's fan of lace is featureless,
A flickering presence only in our minds –
With access, but no tenure which, acknowledged,
Would snare us in the laws of property,
Of traffic, immigration and the rest.

Our peacock stays with us, and is not ours.
By silent nescience we know him best.

A DREAM OF WATER

Glimpsed from the wrong side of a motorway,
Still it was light's best mirror,
Its gleam so startling there
That suddenly to swim came back to me,
Thirst of skin, muscle, nerve for a renewal granted
Wherever to immersion it lay open,
Saline or fresh, in surge, in flow, or quiet,
Even by moonlight, double mirror then,
But to be entered, sensed and penetrated:

Clearest, most alien to warm blood
When snow-fed, from alpine slopes
Or pooled within shallows too fast,
Too rocky for limbs to move;
True to itself peat-coloured in the high moorland beck,
As in hollows it had reclaimed,
The black slate quarry fed by Welsh rain,
Warmer and brownish in Cornwall's claypit ponds;
In lakes not human yet, so wide
That islets, the far shores
Allured like water's wilderness, till trodden;
Like the seas' otherness, when they sustained and killed us
By what they were, each with its moods and weathers:
Current that almost numbed
When air had felt like summer's to one flown in
From a sub-zero north;
The swell that broke reflection;
Stronger, the Biscay undertow
Defied by half-inch lurches
Not for the sake of water, but of land –
So as to look again at light's best mirror.

To concrete, metal, brick
A mirror still, clogged artery of a city,

Could it be more than memory's element here?
The sunlight seen in it left it a river.

Trapped now in alleys where directions lied,
Zigzagging, looping, circling, always diverted
Round a dead centre, away from the blocked-out banks,
I could not reach it. Notices warned
Of penalties for trespass on that in which to drown
Is an archaic mercy. Dry voices jeered:
Who will wash water? With what counter-poisons
The poisoners extract from poisoned earth, air, fire?
Wake up. You're one of them, who will not bathe
Till reason is untangled, the lost ends
Run loose as water at the dream's beginning.

III

THREE ODD SONNETS FROM THE GERMAN

I

ANDREAS GRYPHIUS: HELL

Ah and woe!
Screams! Murder! Wailing! Fear! Cross! Torment! Worms! Indiction!
Pitch! Torture! Hangman! Flame! Stench! Spirits! Cold! Affliction!
End, then, go,
High and low!
Sea! Hillocks! Mountains! Rock! Who can endure such friction?
Engulf it, chasm, gulp down this plaint for dereliction.
Agelong so!
Terrible demons of caves all in darkness / you that both torture
and yourselves are tortured,
Cannot eternity's eternal fire / ever atone for what your evil
has nurtured?
O cruel dread / live death without remission /
This is the flame of perpetual vengeance / fanned by a fury
white-hot and glowing:
Here is the curse of a punishment endless; here is the rage
unremittingly growing:
Perish, mankind! Lest here you know perdition.

(1641. A Baroque sonnet of the Thirty Years' War)

II

CATHARINA VON GREIFFENBERG: ON THE INEFFABLE
INSPIRATION OF THE HOLY SPIRIT

You unseen lightning-flash, you darkly radiant light,
You power that's heart-infused, incomprehensible being!
Something divine within my spirit had its being
That stirs and spurs me: I sense a curious light.

Never by its own power the soul is thus alight.
It was a miracle-wind, a spirit, a creative being,
The eternal power of breath, prime origin of being
That in me kindled for himself this heaven-flaring light.

You mirror-spectrum-glance, you many-coloured gleam!
You glitter to and fro, are incomprehensibly clear;
In truth's own sunlight the spirit-dove-flights gleam.

The God-stirred pool has also been troubled clear!
First on the spirit-sun reflecting it casts its gleam,
The moon; then turns about, and earthward, too, is clear.

(1662)

III

This is the non-existent animal.
Not knowing that, they loved it, loved its ways,
its neck, its posture, loved its quiet gaze
down to the light within it, loved it all.

True, it was *not*. But, because loved, a pure
beast came to be. A space was kept, conceded.
And in that space, left blank for it, secure,
it gently raised its head and hardly needed

to be. They fed it on no kind of corn,
but always only with the right to be.
And on the beast such power this could confer,

its brow put forth new growth. A single horn.
White, it sought out a virgin's company –
and was inside the mirror and in her.

TO A FELLOW POET

(John Montague, for his 60th birthday)

Well past the post that marked no hopes or fears
Because we run no race, but lap the years
Until we drop, and cannot win or lose,
Gasping I stammer out my lack of news:

Brain cells – or data stored by them – grow brittle.
How, then, connect, who recollect so little?
'Cork' and 'Kinsale' I think, but see no place,
Mere aura, not the features of each face
Met there – or was it elsewhere? – as your guest.
But one thing, native to my East, your West,
Palpable, living, shifting, stays with me:
Your gift, tree lupin, carried from your sea
To mine, your garden to my garden, where
It thrives, indifferent to the harsher air;
By now self-seeded, intermarried, too,
With Russell hybrids, purple, pink or blue,
Into whose half-arborean offspring bees
Mixed its faint yellow shades, new subtleties;
(Here sexual surgery mutates no gene
For blossom bigger, gaudier, and obscene)
But more of its true, pallid, moon-cold kind
On small-leaved stalks that straggle, sprawl or wind.

Poems are less transplantable. They draw
On local nutrients, obey a law
Not universal, though to common skies
From their peculiar darknesses they rise.

So out of our long silence, distant friend,
Cut flowers at best, these token rhymes I send
Which, rootless, hardly will outlast the day –
Their function not to be but to convey

Remembered continuities that are all
The running leaves the runners till they fall
Or only pause, drop out beside the track
To breathe unstrained and let the strings go slack.

Such rest between long labours I wish you,
Growth, like your gift's, the circling years renew,
Such wisdom as we need to suffer age
While, true to our folly, still we love and rage.

A PAINTER PAINTED

Lucian Freud: Francis Bacon (1952)

Portrait or *nature morte* or landscape (*nature vivante*) –
Pencil and brush make all a still life, fixed,
So that the wind that swept, breath that came hard
Or easy, when wind has dropped, breath has passed on,
The never visible, may stir again in stillness.

Visible both, the painter and the painted
Passed by me, four decades ago. We met,
We talked, we drank, and we went our ways.
This head's more true than the head I saw.
Closed, these lips tell me more than the lips that spoke.
Lowered, these eyes are better at looking.

A likeness caught? No. *Pictor invenit.*
Slowly, slowly, under his lowered eyelids
He worked, against time, to find the face grown truer,
Coax it to life in paint's dead millimetres,
Compose them into nature, in a light
That is not London's, any hour's or year's;

Furrow it, too, with darkness; let in the winds
That left their roads, painter's and painted's, littered,
Brought branches down, scattering feathers, fruit,
Though for a moment only, stopped the bland flow of breath.

And here it hangs, the still life of a head.

A NOTE ON J.S. BACH

Personality was a distraction
Beyond his means.
No leonine head. No Promethean postures,
Professions, confessions of genius.
A greatness not to be grasped
If you look for it
In anything but the works alone,
The little ones like the great ones.
Odd only in rightness, on any scale,
He excelled himself, always.

Yet of him we learn
That he did write letters other than applications
For appointments, patronage –
To a fellow composer
Early sub-titled 'the Great', to distinguish him
From numerous kin,
Less numerous though it was
Than his untitled colleague's
Prolific not only of music but of musicians.

As jam-jar covers those letters
Served in Couperin's household –
Letters in which for once
Bach must have put into words
Hints at least of self-knowledge,
Tricks of his trade, of the other's,
Points of contact, divergence:
A straw or two, if no more,
To be clutched, magnified, processed
Into musicological coin.

All for jam? But not wasted.
What was useful in them was used.

And that Saxon paper, too, was well made.
The jam was kept, then eaten,
The covers lit a fire.
The secret was given back
To where it belonged, to silence,
Mother and father of music,
Mother and father of words,
Their source and their mouth.

When, at the end, he who, serving, had mastered
Rills, torrents of sound, fountains and oceans,
Presumed to weave into gold the straw of his name –
Oh, the mere surname's four letters, because he could use
    them –
Silence it was that signed for him, broke off the fugue
With an echo of thunder, even the death set to music
Nameless, not his...

HISTORY

Bunk, said the self-made man,
Mass-producer of motors,
And said less and more than he meant:

The past, what was, what happened,
Not the records of that, which are parts,
Man-made, put together
On an assembly line started
Before the invention of wheels;

And made him the self-made man,
Produced the producer, made him
One model, one trademark, one name.

But the whole? Its historian,
All-knowing, does not speak,
Does not write, does not publish,

Forever reserving judgement
On the parts, of motors and men,
On what self-made producers make
Of the records that made them
Make the history they have made:

Bunk? Yes, in part.
And junk – such a clutter
That the last may have no name.

IN THE COUNTRY

1

In May and June, this Election year,
Slugs grew fat as never before
And the little snails, too, took their shares,
Stripping the lupin heads bare,
Quenching the red-hot poker,
Reduced to a slimy stump as it made to rise.

Grey daylight lingered, the summer solstice
Came and passed by.
Nettles grew tall as never before
And cleaver, bindweed proliferated
To strangle what they had not smothered,
Bloated slugs could not swallow
Or cuckoospit cover.

2

As village idiot talk
Sensible people laughed off
Subversive mutters about a Flood:
The Drizzle, you mean, the Long Drizzle,
Is what they said;
But not when they slithered or slipped
On floor tiles that sweated.

3

Nor when the non-Flood's bedraggled Noah
Trying each day to keep seed alive on this earth
For another term, for a season that sunshine would bless,
But soaked to the skin for his pains till dry clothes ran out,
With catarrh and sciatica, pleurisy and pneumonia
Took to his bed in the end.

Empty, his ark drifted off.
Into delirium even no dove bore one sprig or leaf,

4

Though farther afield work was in progress,
Progress at work. They were widening the lanes
For access to the construction site
Of another nuclear power station
Approved for the Heritage Coast,
Next to the Bird Reserve, the protected marshes
Of dwindling wild orchid and meadowsweet.
Costly, of course, retractable eyes could gather
From computer printouts, columns and columns of figures,
The calculations they trust
More than they trust their own senses, their hearts and heads
Or the soul that on Sundays they still may profess to be theirs;
But, in this age of the mollusc, a source
Of profit once more to the greedy feeders;
And, for the moment, no greater danger to them
Than the various poisons on land, in water and air
They believe they are thriving on, in their coats of mucus
Or movable shelters, their shells.

5

All July and August, with breaks as reminders of summer,
Skies remained veiled, the ground sodden.
Neither cherry nor plum could ripen,
But split, then rotted, unpicked.
Great hailstones battered holiday-makers,
Shattered greenhouse roofs.
Near house walls, yield of the nights,
Lay corpses of long-eared bats.

6

The non-Flood's Noah recovered, planning another ark,
Proof against radiation and acid rain,
Air-conditioned, capacious enough to provide for
One breeding pair of every species known to be extant
At the blueprint stage – and, this time, of plants as well.
The question was, who could build it, when such technology
Was reserved for profit-making and war,
When the funds must be raised by private subscription
And that vessel was almost a second Earth.

LIFE AND ART IV

But what rose, Gertrude Stein?
The rose you verbalized was never mine.
Nor is a rose a rose
Till definite by place and kind it grows.
Your triple 'a' rose without shape and colour
Permutes to nothingness, at each turn duller.
I left a hedgerow dog-rose, white and light,
Anyone's flower. The tea-rose in this park,
Though public before dark,
Is no one's when through bars it fades from sight
Into its floral night –
Not yours, not mine, no breeder's and no keeper's,
No homeless walker's, late, no early sleeper's
With bunched unfragrant roses in her room,
Forced from false brightness into curtained gloom.
That rose is not the rose
Which, potted, on a fourth floor balcony shows
One bloom to one who knows
That cash is cash but your cash is not mine:
His tending only made the bought rose shine,
And she for whom he saw it to the hour
When stalk and leaf fulfil themselves, in flower.
Does your tautology
Sprout from a bush or tree,
From any of the ramblers, climbers, creepers?
If less than plastic from a factory,
Metre and rhyme reject what you propose:
Your rose is not a rose is not a rose.

LIFE AND ART V

(Dead Painter to Dead Statesman)

I

Vanity, vanity, whether I speak or keep silence.
All's vanity but the work we did –
Even if that was vain,
If that was done in vanity,
If that was done in vain

Like my portrait of you,
Like the peace you could not win
After a war won.
By you? So your fame would have it.
But it was won by those who, less vain,
Served your purpose and made you great.

'Modern art', you quipped at the presentation,
Sure of obsequious laughter.
What hurt you, though, was a truth
My brush had rendered, your cruel mouth;
And something, too, about greatness
You were not great enough to accept;
So that your widow, ruthless with love and loss,
Did what your greatness forbade you:
Murdered the work, the witness,
Lest they outlive you, lest they embarrass your fame.

Ghostly in monochrome or in specious colours
My portrait dogs your ghost, not mine.
If in vanity both of us lived –
Yes, and painted – the work was not vain.
Ghost among ghosts, my daub remains honest,
Living or dead, like your widow's love.

2

The work, the person, the name –
What chasms divide them!
A silent maker sits at the daily table,
His only care those lines that he cannot trace,
Words that he cannot join, sounds never heard
Until they come to him from the place never searched,
The place that's beyond all searching –
Perhaps to flash, a star extinct
And nameless, their message of light
To receivers unknown, long after.

Or the man, still fleshed and placed,
Is called upon to do this or that
On the strength of his name;
And asks himself: Is it I?
Will the work move the hand again
It made use of before?
Which, for my sort, 'modern',
Makes commissions a thorough rehearsal
For the ghostly part that's yours now and mine.

'Modern'? What can it mean or matter
To us who are out of time?
You, a holiday painter, chose Provence
For landscapes done in the wake
Of painters once 'modern' who worked there.
Worked, not relaxed. That's where the difference lies –
And, no holiday statesman, you knew it.

3

Knew in your heart, even then,
That – employed, commissioned, as I was –
Into your true work's colours you mixed
More than a tinge of the dirt
Which shamelessly now is our world's one pigment.
Round rhetoric and the toff's cigar –
They went down well in wartime;
But the action had to be modern.
Does that leave your work undone?
Not where we are and truth obtains.

If judging were my business,
I should absolve you now,
As I'm absolved of the late commission
By your widow's arson, by love.

LIFE AND ART VI

Misprints in poems, mealy bugs on my grapevines,
Perennial both, however minutely I search,
Pick on them, pluck them out.
For a while they have vanished –
Only to suck the sap, shrivel the clustered fruit,
Yet another vintage disgustingly blackened.
Minuscule both, utterly they destroy
Where, slowly, a pinpoint puncture proves deadly
With a mould that spreads, contamination that oozes
Down invisible ducts into cells that were sound.

AFTER DRYDEN

A few were stirred to witness, though in play,
Love's monomania, deadly for a day,
Shared in a passion that pulled down a pride
And, shaken by the fall, were edified.

Captive spectators, all must now endure
A daily farce, the lines and plot so poor
That those are bored who found disaster funny.
It's called: The World Well Lost – and All for Money.

GOTTHOLD EPHRAIM LESSING:
EPITAPH FOR VOLTAIRE (1779)

Here lies – you pious gentlemen maintain –
One who by rights here long ago should have lain.
In His great mercy may it please
God to forgive his tragedies,
Forgive him, too, his *Henriade*
And all the verselets that he made:
For everything else penned by this one
Was pretty well and ably done.

COMPETITION

(TWO TRAVESTIES)

I

I lisped in numbers, for the numbers game,
And they obeyed, the venal numbers came,
Lined up and breathed by numbers, being tame.
Why not, I thought, when thousands do the same,
Pooling their breath to inflate a single name?
Mine! Mine! Mine! Mine!, massed vanities exclaim,
Mine the divine afflatus, mine the fame
And mine the cash that's fuel to the flame!

Not till my lines limped home to me, gone lame,
Not till they'd failed me, was I touched by shame,
But to the judges shifted all the blame:
Oh, my good chimers, packed within a frame,
My marching marksmen, true to their one aim,
Dear mercenaries whom deaf ears could maim!

I lisped in numbers, but my numbers came
Nowhere near first in that year's numbers game.
More games will follow, different, yet the same
Until computers pick the lucky name –
And for rich rhyming grant me rich acclaim.

2

British poets, know your place,
Confined, with little living-space
On the circuit, on the papers,
No room at all for bardic capers.
Know: the market now is tough.
Play it safe, but play it rough.
On your own you'll not succeed:
Well oiled PR, that's what you need,
Teamwork in the pubs and clubs
Where each operator rubs
Shoulders with a kindred spirit,
Kindred in graft, if not in merit,
Skill, inspiration and the rest –
A load of bookish cant at best,
Now that your brand name and your image
Alone will see you through the scrimmage.

British poets, know your friends,
Praise whatever serves your ends.
Puncture with a knowing sneer
Those who put truth before career
Although a knowing silence would
Keep such presumption out, for good.
That lesson learnt, don't worry much:
You'll have what counts, the common touch,
And, known to have it, need not shun
Consistently the ingenious pun,
Recondite fancy or allusion,
Ellipse, analogy and fusion,
Lapse into vision even, or
At least the puzzling metaphor
Which in another's book would be
Abominable artistry.

MR LITTLEJOY'S AFTER-DINNER SPEECH

Mad dams and sires, though unaccustomed quite
To public squeaking, squeak I must tonight –
With slops of the ting? – on the diminished pate
Of our poor realm and steeple, duped of late.
Tie-tongued, I burrow from the bord of Ire:
Churning and churning in the deepening mire
The managed cannot hear the manager
Or versy visa, while, more's what, and sinister,
He, she or it's a synonym for Minister.
Pings fall athwart, the centre cannot hold
For client-voters, buying what they're sold:
Disjecta membra, infinitesimal shares
In the wacked commonhealth which, whole, was theirs.
The Shop of State? Alas, no slip or quip
Where salesmanshop has ousted statesmanship.
Consumer choice? A precious freedom, brother –
With luck, between one rip-off and another,
Choice of contaminations, that to come,
Processed and packaged, dumped upon the dumb
Who for the advertisement, not the product, pay
Till for the next, more botched, that's put away...
Pipe down? Shut up? All right. I've sad my hay.

MR LITTLEJOY CONSIDERS HIS ESTATE

Be prudent, providential? Make a will?
Give myself heirs before, more gaga still,
I jumble my name's letters and the date?
It's not on my account that I hesitate.

Yes, there's the house, historically curious,
Most curious for the leaks in it, decay
In rafters, window-frames, the joints and gulleys
Not to be mended. If each rainy day,
Now mutely, now vociferously furious,
I run for bowls to catch the splash and spray,
Wipe my drenched papers – I, the fool who chose it –
How to a loved one can I leave my follies,
Pass on that house and with a will impose it?
And yet the continuity is all:
This listed, twisted, patched, botched, cracked, pocked wall,
This roof that sags but somehow does not fall
As beetles do, and wood dust, from the beams,
With muck of ages from the widening seams:
Keep that, and it is drudgery you inherit,
Exasperations and anxiety dreams.
Sell up, and you'll betray it to the schemes
Of some improver who will kill the spirit.

Worse, there's the plot that was a garden, neat,
Lawn bare, unbroken save by garden seat,
The one long border lined with low box hedges,
No trees but for a windbreak round the edges,
And fruit-trees in the orchard, useful trees
Hedged once again, for shelter, and to please
With the same symmetry a stricter taste –
Half-wilderness now, more wooded and more waste,
Richer and more intractable, lush and harsh
With weeds allowed to immigrate from the marsh;

Sown or transplanted even; then, if rare,
Tended and fended with a gardener's care
Who now forgets how much is nature there,
How much design, but labours to maintain
A mutable rightness he could not explain
Or delegate; arranges and selects,
And, where he feels he must, uproots, rejects...
No, where and when he can; that's less and less.
Oh, and on land so impatient to regress
That brief neglect leaves total wilderness,
Rubbery bindweed, cleaver nets embroil
Frail shoots constricted, throttled by their coil,
Seldom he sits or walks without the need
To save the endangered, check the greed and speed
Of grosser plants, abort their spreading seed.

And there's unreal estate, the literary,
Still to be managed, and by one as wary,
Uncompromising as those have to be
Who sift the real from unreality.
Am I to posit that from my remains
A living will accrue? Pass on the pains
And the presumption, in the hope of earning
Doles from that grindstone posthumously turning?
Executor? Appointing him, her, them,
To execution such I should condemn –
And slow at that, when usury's attrition,
Not use or making, is the true condition
Of all exchange and commerce, computation
Fills the redundancy of head and heart.
Who'll need their dark collusions, fusions – art?

Like the loved plot, to love and cultivation
Or dissolution and abandonment
I leave the work that was not willed but lent,
The words no more my own than is the land
Which, served, could serve me with rewards unplanned,
Discoveries, conjunctions, harmonies:

For these I worked, and for no joys but these.
List them? Apportion them? Relieve their lack
With my residual assets, bric-à-brac?
Dearly I wish them my most near and dear,
My known and unknown friends – all nameless here.

CODICIL

Nothing I owned but what owned me,
Nothing possessed but what possessed me.
Found, you will find it, and will be
    Where, yours, it can attest me.

MR LITTLEJOY'S PRAYER

Logos, one Word before the world was peopled,
Take back your progeny of words, words, words
Whose babbling intercourse, proliferation
Makes counterworlds, more packed than tube trains are
When offices close, with some not even sure
Of a mere dosshouse bed; and with no Malthus
To warn, far less to legislate, against
Their polymorphous promiscuity.
Oh, and immortal, thanks to tablet, paper,
Translator, necromancer, necrophil
For whom the living are not good enough,
Too mixed, too lax, too ugly or too blank.
In ever-growing graveyards, libraries,
Once more they copulate and grossly breed,
Dead with the dead or living with the dead.
Contain them Logos, curb the lexic mob.

If now I speak, it is to clear a space
Where things are things, grow nameless in your name.

Be in that narrow silence, Word, and fill it.

IV
Dream Poems

LITERARY

A fellow scribbler shows me his latest poem,
Hands me the sheet
And the letters, too small to read with the naked eye,
Are moving indeed: mites
That crawl here and there, shifty,
One or two right over the edge of the paper.
Does it matter, I ask, if they disappear?
No, he says, there are others to take their places.

Through strong lenses I can follow
Their permutations, lively enough, suggestive,
Recoiling only when the more sinister kinds
Leave the page and threaten my skin.

Best of my books, I have never read it,
Only from dream to dream gathered
That somewhere it had appeared –
Pirated, decades ago,
Verse or prose picked up
By someone wiser than I from work I'd mislaid, forgotten.

On my own shelves I have found a copy,
The cover so faded,
The title so rubbed that barely I could make out:
DIARY OF THE GODFATHERED. Not mine! Not mine!
But the name was above it, in durable type.

Never now I shall read it.
Posthumous from the start,
It was always beyond me,
Its coherence that of the dark,
Its light not that I can see by
But unbroken, undiffused.

Let it slip again into lostness
Behind recognizable spines.

SHORT STORY

There was this house where each in his own fashion,
Each with his fancy's furniture could work and sleep;
Whether as commune, corporation, co-operative
Founded, we never asked. By looseness it cohered
For those who came and went, though none spoke much of
    sharing
Or of division. Somehow the rates were paid,
The premises maintained, outgoings met.

Suddenly ceilings cracked, stair boards were rotten,
Work tables broke their legs, light bulbs exploded.
If now between apartments one inmate ran
Into another, it was to blame or curse him.
Much worse, the stray dogs of the city had picked out
The precincts for their terrain, covered the doormat even
With turds and drips and vomit. 'Where there's muck there's
    money',
The caretaker said; and: 'Clean your own rooms!'.
How could we, when daily we carried in
The stench and the pollution? Oh, we renovated,
But could not work alone nor work together,
The bills piled up, we could not bear each other
Since all of us reeked, and all of us were sick.

There was this house. It's been demolished now.

ON DUTY

Attending the telephone
I take to be still connected
To some headquarters or other
Become expert in reticence,
I try to remember the old war
I joined up for, but can't get beyond
The trestle bed I rose from
This morning, any morning,
In a barrack room shared with no one;
And can't be sure when it was
That a bugle inside my head,
Blowing reveille, became
The blare that roused me from nightmare
At the moment of sudden awareness
That years or decades have passed
Since my parents answered a letter,
Of the flash in darkness showing me
The girl I was to have married
Smile to herself undecided
Between two bedroom doors,
Each with a man behind it.
Awake, must ask myself,
Man? Is the designation current?
If ever again a voice
Should come through, will it use
Human, obsolete words
To charge, discharge me
Whose number, rank, name
Were dropped long ago
From records transferred to computers,
And leave this table real,
This pen, the blank forms?

Or is silence not only the code
But the message I'm here to receive
And pass on, undeciphered?
Pass on to whom, though, to whom?

RECOVERY

To swim I had gone out,
Towards noon, in hot weather.

With four diseases, my clothes mislaid or stolen,
By nightfall I crawled the streets.

If I lay low, I was done for.
If I showed myself, naked, what then?

There was this rag of towel
And I could not give in.

From behind dustbins, skips,
I dragged myself to a door –

Of a shed, it seemed, workshop or store,
For directions at best, mediation.

The woman laughed, but she let me in.
I looked, and the place was a ward.

'It's made up, for you', she said,
Laughing still, pointing

To the first bed on the right.
'Youl'll need no loincloth here.

Nor more rest than it takes to tell
Which illness it is you'd have died of.

By then there'll be light again
For you to go home by, healed.'

THE TRAY

About to go home, discharged
From this dormitory, barrack room
That for years I had shared
With fellows not of my choosing,
By a bed not mine I caught sight
Of my heirloom, forgotten tray
Inset with ancient tiles
Most rarely patterned and glazed.
'Mine', I said to the orderly,
'I shall be taking it with me.'

As I touched it, I saw the face
Of him who had used it.
'The colours, lines that so please me',
I read in the gaze met,
'For him too, are themselves;
Please him, and pleased all these
Whom I leave to their dying,
Whom I leave to die.
To our death in life I'll leave it,
The thing dead and alive.'

New to me, shining, the tray consented.

ENDLESS

It began as a couch-grass root,
Stringy and white,
Straggling, to no end,
Branching out, breaking
For procreation.

Traced and pulled, it became
A bramble shoot that climbed
Through leafage of shrub, tree
With a root at its tip, for plunging.

I pulled at it, pulled,
Miles of the thing came away,
More and more.

I pulled and pulled until
I saw that now
Straight up it had risen
With its end in space,
With a root in heaven.

DREAM

It looked like a parting. Back into youth
You went from me, one hand around the hand
Of a small girl who, skipping, tugged you on
Towards a May-time meadow; in the other carried
The flute you have not played for twenty-five years.

Work tied me down; and what I worked on was
Intricate preparations for appointments fixed
In city offices that administer death.

Pale wintry sunrays glinted on your hair
And on the child's, of the same colour as yours.
From the dark house I could not even wave

But never doubted: wherever it might be
That once again a tune came from the flute
I should be there to hear it – the same air
You played for me when first we met, and parted
Till in a circle all our journeys turned.